THE EARTH IS FLAT!

Science Facts and Fictions

Library of Congress Cataloging-in-Publication Data
Atkinson, Mary, 1966-
    The Earth is flat! : science facts and fictions / by Mary Atkinson.
        p. cm. -- (Shockwave)
    Includes index.
    ISBN-10: 0-531-17580-4 (lib. bdg.)
    ISBN-13: 978-0-531-17580-4 (lib. bdg.)
    ISBN-10: 0-531-18812-4 (pbk.)
    ISBN-13: 978-0-531-18812-5 (pbk.)
    1. Errors, Scientific--Juvenile literature.
    2. Science--History--Popular works--Juvenile literature.
    3. Astronomy--History--Popular works--Juvenile literature.
    4. Physics--History--Popular works--Juvenile literature.
    5. Earth--Figure--Juvenile literature. I. Title.

    Q172.5.E77A85 2007
    500--dc22

2007019983

Published in 2008 by Children's Press, an imprint of Scholastic Inc.,
557 Broadway, New York, New York 10012
www.scholastic.com

SCHOLASTIC, CHILDREN'S PRESS, and associated logos are trademarks
and/or registered trademarks of Scholastic Inc.

08 09 10 11 12 13 14 15 16 17
10 9 8 7 6 5 4 3 2 1

Printed in China through Colorcraft Ltd., Hong Kong

Author: Mary Atkinson
Educational Consultant: Ian Morrison
Editor: Mary Atkinson
Designer: Matthew Alexander
Photo Researcher: Jamshed Mistry

Photographs by: Big Stock Photo (scientist, p. 25); ©**David Young-Wolff/PhotoEdit**
(roller skater, p. 23); **Emerald City/Minden** (p. 26); **Gary Borkan/rare-posters.com**
(Alhazen, p. 15); **Getty Images** (p. 7; p. 28); **Ingram Image Library** (dolphin, p. 12);
Jennifer and Brian Lupton (teenagers, pp. 32–33); **Photolibrary** (p. 8; p. 10; Maya myth,
p. 11; p. 13; Ali Sufi, p. 15; trial of Galileo, p. 17; pp. 18–19; Robert Boyle, p. 21; p. 22;
Newton, p. 23; p. 27; pp. 29–31; horsehead nebula, pp. 32–33); **Popperfoto** (Aristotle,
p. 12); **Tranz: Corbis** (cover; p. 3; Ferdinand Magellan, p. 11; p. 14; p. 16; Galileo's test,
p. 17; p. 20; alchemists, p. 21; p. 24; basketball player, p. 25)

All illustrations and other photographs © Weldon Owen Education Inc.

SHOCKWAVE
SCIENCE

THE EARTH IS FLAT!

Science Facts and Fictions

Mary Atkinson

children's press®

An imprint of Scholastic Inc.
NEW YORK • TORONTO • LONDON • AUCKLAND • SYDNEY
MEXICO CITY • NEW DELHI • HONG KONG
DANBURY, CONNECTICUT

CHECK THESE OUT!

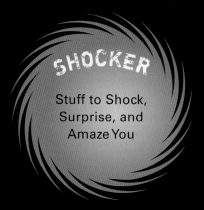

SHOCKER

Stuff to Shock,
Surprise, and
Amaze You

Quick Recaps
and Notable
Notes

Word Stunners
and Other Oddities

The Heads-Up
on Expert Reading

Links to More
Information

CONTENTS

HIGH-POWERED WORDS	6
GET ON THE WAVELENGTH	8
Myths and Knowledge	10
Aristotle: The Great Thinker	12
Information Lost and Reclaimed	14
Galileo's Crime	16
Medical Mysteries	18
From Alchemy to Chemistry	20
The Scientific Revolution	22
Scientific Thinking	24
Scientific Method	26
Beware: Take Care!	28
The Edge of Knowledge	30
AFTERSHOCKS	32
GLOSSARY	34
FIND OUT MORE	35
INDEX	36
ABOUT THE AUTHOR	36

assume to accept that something is true without checking it

gravity the force that pulls objects toward the center of the earth

hypothesis (*hye POTH uh siss*) a proposed explanation, which can be tested, of why or how something happens

observation close examination of and attention to something

phenomena (*fe NOM uh nuh*) events or facts that can be seen, felt, or experienced

physicist (*FIZ uh sist*) someone who studies physics, which is the science of matter and energy

theory an idea, which has been tested experimentally, about why or how something happens

· ·

For additional vocabulary, see Glossary on page 34.

Many words ending in *-is* form plurals by replacing the *-is* with *-es*, for example: *hypothesis/hypotheses, axis/axes, analysis/analyses,* and *oasis/oases.*

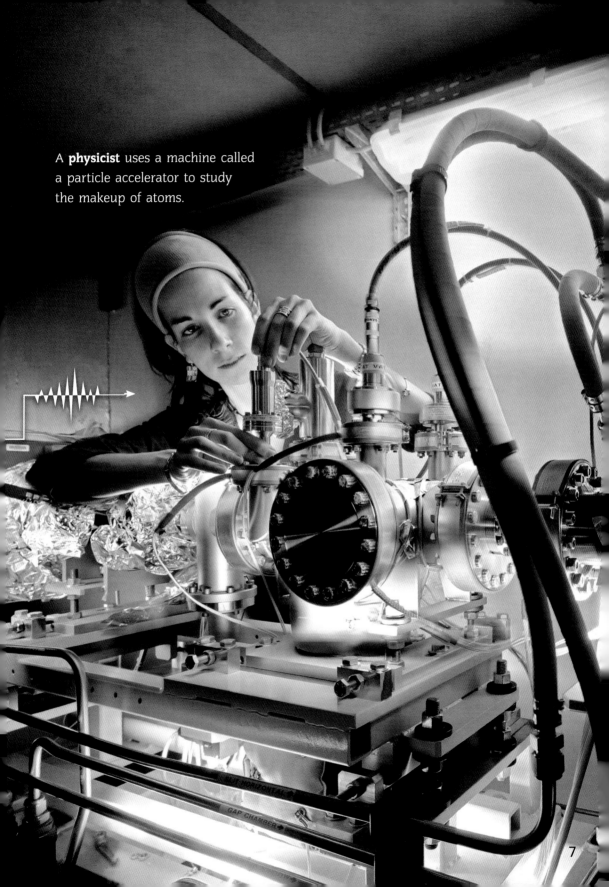

A **physicist** uses a machine called a particle accelerator to study the makeup of atoms.

In ancient times, many people thought that the world was flat. Some people thought that if you traveled too far, you might fall off. However, by 240 B.C., the Greek **astronomer** Eratosthenes (*AIR uh TOSS thuh neez*) had figured out that our planet is **spherical**. He had even figured out a rough measurement for the **circumference** of the earth. By 100 A.D., many educated people in places such as Europe, North Africa, and the Middle East knew that the earth was spherical.

By the 1600s, the big question was whether or not the earth was the center of the universe. People debated fiercely on both sides of the argument. Then, as now, people had trouble knowing which new ideas were right and which were wrong.

This map of the known world was created in 1472. It was drawn using information written by the Greek astronomer Ptolemy (*TAHL uh mee*) in about 150 A.D. Ptolemy believed that the earth was spherical.

Curved lines indicate that the earth is spherical.

It is easy to laugh at the mistakes people made in the past. However, it is harder to sort fact from fiction when ideas are new. It is especially difficult if the new ideas don't match our existing beliefs. Over the last few centuries, scientists have tried to work in **logical** ways to make their **theories** as likely as possible to be true. However, each theory lasts only until someone comes up with a slightly better one. Our understanding of the universe is increased one new theory at a time.

GREAT MISTAKES

Scientists make many mistakes on the way to discovering the truth. Take a look at these quotes.

I do not think that the wireless waves [radio waves] I have discovered will have any practical application.
Heinrich Hertz, German **physicist** (1888)

X-rays will prove to be a hoax.
Lord Kelvin, British physicist (1899)

Louis Pasteur's theory of germs is ridiculous fiction.
Pierre Pachet, French science professor (1872)

I am bold enough to say that a manmade moon voyage will never occur.
Dr. Lee de Forest, U.S. inventor (1926)

Space travel is utter bilge [garbage].
Richard Woolley, British Astronomer Royal (1956)

MYTHS AND KNOWLEDGE

People have always wondered about the world around them. Early people wanted to know why the sun moved across the sky. They wondered where the first life came from. One of the ways they answered these questions was with stories, or myths. In the ancient stories of many cultures, gods and goddesses caused the things that happened in nature. We can discover what questions were important to people in the past by reading their myths. For example, many cultures have creation myths. These stories recount how the earth and the first people came to exist.

As people started to farm and trade, they needed information about time and **navigation**. Many ancient peoples studied the stars to help create calendars and locate their positions. Over the centuries, much of that knowledge has been lost. As a result, we don't know when or where some discoveries were first made. The first discoveries are often taken as those for which we have the earliest well-known evidence.

An Egyptian creation ▶ myth from more than 3,000 years ago tells of the gods that make up the universe. Shu, the air god, separates Nut, the sky goddess, from Geb, the earth god. The sun god, Ra, travels over the sky, which is seen as a heavenly river.

The creation myth of the Maya people of Central America is called *Popol Vuh*. It tells how the god, Heart of Sky, created people. His first attempts to make people, from mud and then from wood, both failed. But his final attempt, to make people from corn, was a success.

In 1521, Portuguese explorer ▶ Ferdinand Magellan became the first European to cross the Pacific Ocean. His journey has gone down in history as a great feat of navigation. However, he was not the first person to navigate the Pacific Ocean. Pacific Islanders had been crossing it for centuries before Magellan.

ARISTOTLE: THE GREAT THINKER

Modern science probably grew from ideas that began in Egypt and Babylonia (modern-day Iraq). These ideas inspired the ancient Greek **philosophers**. One of those Greek philosophers, Aristotle (*AR is staht uhl*), had a particularly lasting influence on European scientific thinking.

Aristotle lived mainly in Greece from 384 B.C. to 322 B.C. He wrote on many topics, including science. He developed ways of logical thinking that are still used today. Unfortunately, he didn't believe in experiments. He and other Greek philosophers felt that experiments were lowly and that people should use their intellect instead. He relied mainly on common sense and, as a starting point, **observation**. This led to many errors.

◄ Aristotle classified more than 500 animal species. He listed them in groups, such as those that give birth to live young and those that lay eggs. He was a careful observer. He noted that dolphins give birth to live young, so he grouped them with land animals, rather than with fish.

Alexander the Great

Aristotle

▲
Aristotle once tutored Alexander, the prince of Macedonia. Among other things, he taught him the art of powerful public speaking. Alexander later conquered much of the land between North Africa and India. In doing so, he spread Greek ideas to other places. Alexander is now known as Alexander the Great.

DID YOU KNOW?

Aristotle Summary
- Greek philosopher
- developed ways of logical thinking
- classified more than 500 species
- didn't believe in experimentation
- tutored Alexander the Great

SOME THINGS ARISTOTLE GOT WRONG

- You can't make green by mixing other colors.
- Heavy objects fall faster than light ones.
- The function of the brain is to cool the blood.

INFORMATION
LOST AND RECLAIMED

The ancient Romans studied and revered the works of the ancient Greeks. But when the Roman Empire fell in 476 A.D., Europe went into a period sometimes called the Dark Ages. Much information was lost or forgotten. However, scholars in the Middle East preserved many of the works of Greek philosophers. These scholars traveled to Persia (modern-day Iran and Afghanistan) and to India, where they gathered more ideas. They advanced scientific knowledge with many accurate observations.

In about 1200, new **translations** of Aristotle's works were introduced to Europe. Aristotle's writings became popular. People thought that they held great wisdom. During the **Renaissance**, Europeans began to search for more writings from ancient Greece and Rome. At first, many Europeans thought that the knowledge of the ancient Greeks could never be improved upon.

◀ In Alexandria, in Egypt, there was a library that contained copies of all the known scrolls of the time. It had more than 500,000 scrolls. Sadly, the library was destroyed in war in the late 200s A.D. None of its contents have survived.

The Egyptian city of Alexandria is named after Alexander the Great. Even though it bears his name, Alexander never lived to see the completed city.

The Arab scientist Alhazen studied the way light rays bend when they go into different **mediums**. He showed that light goes from an object to the eye. The ancient Greek scientist Ptolemy had thought that light went from the eyes to the object. We now know that Alhazen was right.

The great Arab astronomer Al Sufi ▶ studied the Greek astronomer Ptolemy. In 964, he published a book listing the position, size, and color of about 1,018 stars.

GALILEO'S CRIME

In the past, people thought that Earth was the center of the universe. The first person to question this was Nicolaus Copernicus, a Polish astronomer. In 1543, he wrote that Earth **orbited** the sun in perfect circles. His theory wasn't completely correct, but it was the best theory at the time. In 1609, German astronomer Johannes Kepler studied new data on the motions of the planets. From this information, he calculated that the planets orbit the sun in **elliptical** paths.

The Italian scientist Galileo Galilei could see that Kepler's theory made sense. He started publicizing the information. Church leaders thought this new idea made Earth less important and went against their teachings. Galileo was eventually imprisoned for refusing to take back his beliefs.

Galileo realized that ▶ to do experiments, scientists needed tools. He improved the telescope and used it to look at the stars. He noticed that Jupiter was orbited by several moons. This was more evidence that Earth was not the center of the universe.

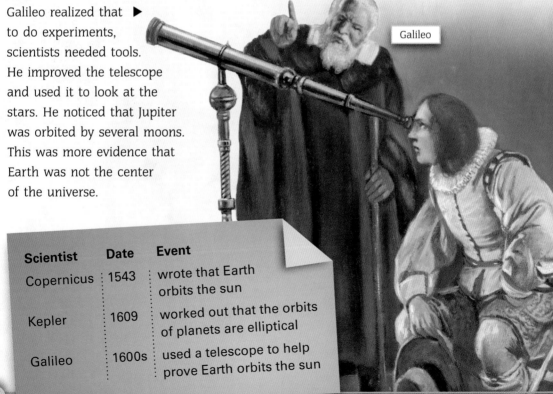

Galileo

Scientist	Date	Event
Copernicus	1543	wrote that Earth orbits the sun
Kepler	1609	worked out that the orbits of planets are elliptical
Galileo	1600s	used a telescope to help prove Earth orbits the sun

DID YOU KNOW?

Today, math is often used to calculate scientific results. Galileo also used math in his experiments. However, in his time, it was considered poor form to mix math and science. In his official writings, Galileo downplayed how much math he used.

▲

Galileo was prosecuted in 1633. Then, in 1992, 359 years later, the Roman Catholic Church apologized for having treated him wrongly!

▼

Galileo believed in experimentation. He tested Aristotle's idea that heavy objects fall faster than light ones. He found that this "common sense" idea was not true. Weight does not affect the speed of a falling object.

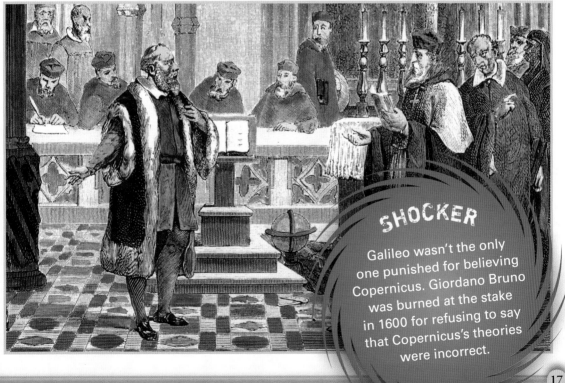

SHOCKER

Galileo wasn't the only one punished for believing Copernicus. Giordano Bruno was burned at the stake in 1600 for refusing to say that Copernicus's theories were incorrect.

MEDICAL MYSTERIES

I t was Hippocrates, a Greek **physician** born in 460 B.C., who first came up with the idea that diseases might have natural causes. He was the first person to study medicine as a science. However, it was probably Empedocles (*em PED uh klees*), a philosopher from Sicily, who initially had the biggest impact on medicine. In the 400s B.C., he decided that the world was made of only four "roots," or elements: fire, air, earth, and water. These were later linked to four supposed **humors** of the body: blood, yellow bile, black bile, and **phlegm**.

No experiments were done to prove this theory. However, in the 100s A.D, it was taken up enthusiastically by Galen (*GAY luhn*), a Greek physician. He decided that if a person was feverish, he or she must have too much fire. Since fire was believed to be linked to blood, he thought that the cure was to drain blood from the body. Bloodletting was very popular right through the Middle Ages. Unfortunately, it killed far more people than it cured.

Bloodletting in the Middle Ages

The pronunciation guides for *Empedocles* and *Galen* really help. If I had to spend time trying to figure these out, it would slow me down and affect my understanding.

▲

Unlike many others in his time, Galen did perform some experiments. He cut up corpses of dead animals to study how bodies work. He gave lectures about his discoveries. His writing on anatomy became the standard medical textbook in many parts of the world until the 1500s.

In the Middle Ages, doctors used ▶ blood-sucking leeches for bloodletting. Today, some doctors are again using leeches. They use them to drain wounds. Doctors also use a drug (right) made from leeches to treat blood-clotting problems.

FROM ALCHEMY TO CHEMISTRY

In Egypt, in the 300s A.D., some people believed that metals such as lead and mercury could be turned into gold. This process was called alchemy. It was based on an idea by Aristotle called transmutation. Alchemists believed that they could change substances into other substances by changing their balance of air, water, fire, and earth.

Alchemy was popular in Europe until the 1600s. Some rulers made alchemy illegal because they feared it would make other people richer than they were. The alchemists carried on in secret, but they never did succeed. We now know that this is because gold is a basic element. It can't be made by mixing other substances.

One valuable thing that alchemists did, however, was experiment. Out of alchemy came chemistry. Chemistry is the study of substances and how they mix. At first, chemistry was considered a lowly science. It was tainted by the reputation of alchemy and not taken seriously.

◀ Some incorrect science theories have led scientists to the truth. In the 1700s, two German scientists came up with a new theory that was completely wrong. They believed that materials give off an invisible gas called phlogiston (*flo JISS tuhn*) when they burn. They thought phlogiston put out flames in airtight containers. The theory explained many observations, but phlogiston was never found to exist. However, the theory did lead other chemists to discover oxygen and carbon dioxide.

◀ Alchemists had laboratories. They used all kinds of equipment to grind, heat, and separate substances. Over time, the equipment they used developed into the equipment used by modern chemists.

Irish scientist Robert Boyle (1627–1691) was one of the first modern chemists. He is famous for his experiments with gases. It was Boyle who finally disproved the theory of the four basic elements. ▼

DID YOU KNOW? Modern scientists have discovered that transmutation does happen in nature. Some radioactive atoms release part of their **nucleus** and so become different elements. For example, a uranium atom can release part of its nucleus and become thorium.

THE SCIENTIFIC REVOLUTION

In the late 1600s, huge breakthroughs started happening in science. Isaac Newton was an English scientist working at about the same time as Robert Boyle. In 1687, Newton published a book that changed science forever. He came up with the laws of motion and the law of **gravity**. Together, these ideas described how objects on Earth move, and why planets and moons orbit larger objects. He showed that a few basic laws can be used to describe the universe. Even today, most scientists use these laws in their calculations. However, Newton wasn't completely right.

Newton thought that time was constant. He also thought that space was fixed. It wasn't until the early 1900s that scientist Albert Einstein realized that neither of these things is true. He discovered that Newton's theories don't hold true in some situations, such as when an object is moving nearly at the speed of light.

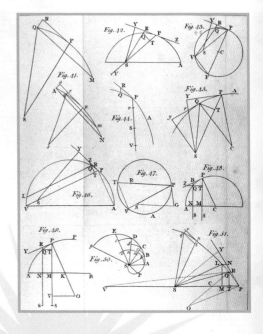

In order to work out his theories, ▶ Newton needed to use complicated mathematics. He used **geometry** (right) from a book written by Euclid (*YU klid*), an ancient Greek philosopher. He also had to invent a completely new kind of math called calculus.

Newton discovered the force of gravity after watching an apple fall from a tree. He realized that the force that pulled the apple to the ground is the same force that keeps the moon orbiting Earth.

NEWTON'S LAWS OF MOTION

1. An object moves in a straight line or stays at rest unless a force acts on it.

2. How much an object accelerates depends on its mass and how much force is applied to it.

3. Forces act in pairs. Every action has an equal and opposite reaction.

According to the first of Newton's laws (above), this skateboarder would keep going forever with just one push if the force of **friction** didn't slow her down.

SCIENTIFIC THINKING

Today, we tend to think of science as the logical study of nature and the universe. However, this concept of science developed slowly over time. In the early 1900s, Karl Popper, an Austrian philosopher of science, started thinking about the nature of "real science." He thought that science should be based on known facts. He thought that a scientific theory should be able to be tested. He said that some things, such as **astrology**, are not based entirely on logic and known facts. This doesn't mean that they can't be true, it just means that they aren't sciences.

Modern scientists usually publish their theories and experimental results. They write up exactly how they did their experiments and what they think the results mean. This allows other scientists to study their ideas and repeat the experiments. To publish or not to publish is the dilemma that faces a scientist with a new theory. Publication could mean fame and glory. It could also mean that the theory will soon be proven wrong.

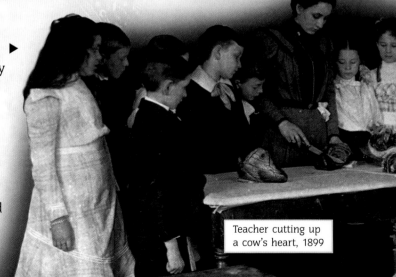

In the early 1800s, most ▶ schools taught geography and some even taught navigation. However, the main subjects were English, Latin, math, and history. It was not until the late 1800s that many schools considered science important.

Teacher cutting up a cow's heart, 1899

▲
Modern scientists perform their experiments carefully. They also keep accurate notes of their results. Each experiment is performed many times before the scientist feels sure that the results are correct.

Popper thought that scientific theories should be based on a kind of logic called deductive reasoning. He felt that too many theories were based on chains of a less reliable logic called inductive reasoning.

DEDUCTIVE REASONING

This is a thought process that leads you to a conclusion that must be true if the observations it is based on are correct. Here is an example.

There are three basketballs in the gym.
There are two basketballs in the closet.
There are no other basketballs in the school.
Therefore, there are five basketballs in the school.

INDUCTIVE REASONING

This is a thought process that is probably true, but not definitely. Here is an example.

Ruby loves basketball.
She has played basketball after school every day this year. Therefore, Ruby will play basketball after school today.

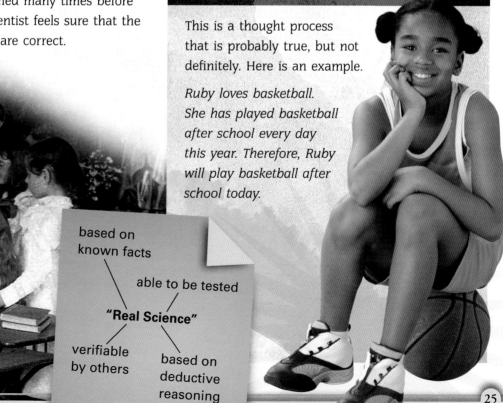

based on known facts

able to be tested

"Real Science"

verifiable by others

based on deductive reasoning

SCIENTIFIC METHOD

T oday, scientists often follow a particular process to reach their conclusions. It is called the scientific method. It can be used in many situations. Here is an example.

You have <u>observed</u> a bird eating some sunflower seeds. From this, you form a **hypothesis** that this kind of bird likes sunflower seeds. You <u>predict</u> that it will eat more sunflower seeds if it gets the chance. Then you create an <u>experiment</u> to test the hypothesis. You put some sunflower seeds in a bird feeder. The results indicate that your hypothesis is correct because the bird eats the seeds. One day, you leave out sesame seeds instead. The bird eats them. From this observation, you revise, or improve, your hypothesis: The bird likes seeds of various types. This new hypothesis now needs testing.

THE SCIENTIFIC METHOD

1. Observation
(Observe something you'd like to understand better.)

▼

2. Create a Hypothesis
(Come up with a possible explanation
for your observation.)

▼

3. Prediction
(Note what you think will happen in a particular
situation if your hypothesis is correct.)

▼

4. Experiment
(Perform an experiment to test the prediction.)

5. Results Do Not Match Prediction
(Go back and come up with
a revised hypothesis.)

5. Results Match Prediction
(Do more experiments to be sure.
Then publish your new theory.)

Not all hypotheses are easy to test. Some are too dangerous or too expensive. Sometimes scientists make models. These scientists are using a model to study soil **erosion** without harming the environment. In other situations, scientists use computers to **simulate** a real situation.

This scientist is collecting **bacteria** for an experiment. She will see if they can survive the conditions in space. She wants to test a hypothesis that bacteria on meteorites could travel from one planet to another.

DID YOU KNOW?

Without the wrong theories, we would never get to the ones that work. Science thrives on mistakes, and fortunately, there have been plenty of them.

BEWARE: TAKE CARE!

Scientists do experiments because they want to find out more about something. Sometimes this has led to danger. For example, Marie Curie worked with radioactive chemicals in the early 1900s. She made some important discoveries, but she didn't realize how dangerous radioactive materials can be. She died at age sixty-seven of cancer. Many think that her cancer was caused by her working with radioactivity without the proper protection. Marie Curie earned two Nobel prizes for her work. She also helped make radiotherapy treatment available to cancer patients. Unfortunately, these advances came along too late to save her own life.

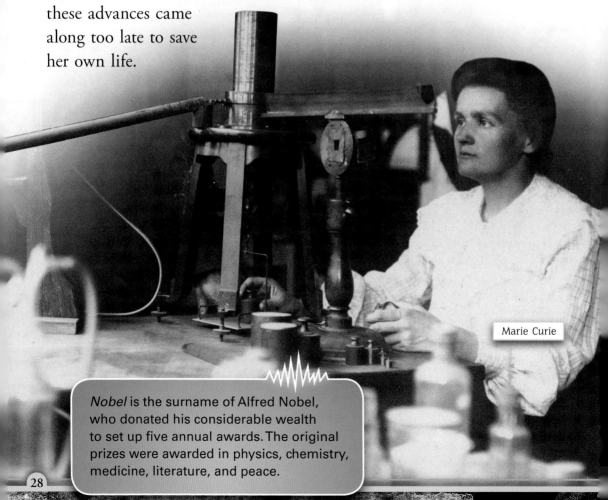

Marie Curie

Nobel is the surname of Alfred Nobel, who donated his considerable wealth to set up five annual awards. The original prizes were awarded in physics, chemistry, medicine, literature, and peace.

Sometimes people **assume** that scientists know more than they do. If scientists say that they have no proof that something is dangerous, some people think this means that scientists know that it is safe. This is not necessarily the case.

> **SURGEON GENERAL'S WARNING:** Smoking Causes Lung Cancer, Heart Disease, and Emphysema, and May Complicate Pregnancy.

▲
For many years, scientists said that there was no proof that smoking was bad for human health. Some people thought that this meant that smoking was safe. Sadly, they were wrong. Experiments have since shown that smoking increases the chances of getting several deadly diseases.

◄
Sometimes scientific research doesn't happen until after a problem arises. It was not until many animals had been poisoned that scientists performed experiments to look into the dangerous side effects of the pesticide DDT. DDT was finally banned in the 1970s, almost 30 years after it came on the market. These days, responsible companies have their products scientifically tested before they sell them.

THE EDGE OF KNOWLEDGE

Scientists don't have all the answers. Not even the great physicist Albert Einstein knew everything. He spent a great deal of time searching for an equation that would link the main **phenomena** in the universe. He wanted a link between electricity, magnetism, and gravity, but he never found it.

Einstein wanted to believe that every outcome could be predicted scientifically. He didn't think that anything happened by chance. Today, some physicists believe that atoms and the things that make up atoms behave in ways that depend on probability and statistics. For example, if an electron can follow two different paths, we cannot predict for sure which path it will take. Some people think that this means that the future is not already decided, and that we have choices.

Einstein is famous for writing, "I am, at all events, convinced that [God] does not play dice with the universe." This referred to his belief that nothing happened by chance.

Scientists and students often imagine atoms as looking like this. We now know that this is not what atoms actually look like. However, we continue to use this model because it helps students understand many chemical reactions.

▼

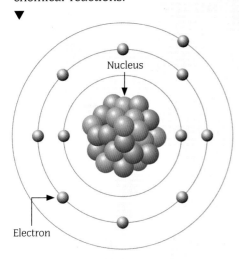

Nucleus

Electron

Atoms are probably more like this. The electrons behave a bit like waves and a bit like particles. The dark areas show where the electrons are most likely to be at any given moment.

▼

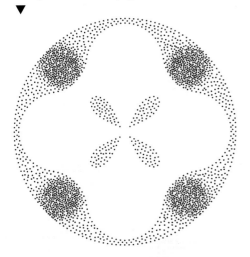

Michael Green, English physicist, studying string theory

▲

Some physicists are now investigating an idea called string theory. Like Einstein, they are trying to find a theory of everything. Their work is complex and very difficult for most people to understand. Their theories involve extremely tiny rolls of ten-dimensional pieces of space-time.

Our knowledge of the universe has come a long way since the days when people thought that the earth was flat. Now scientists are trying to work out the nature of the universe itself. String-theory scientists are investigating the extremely tiny particles that make up atoms.

WHAT DO YOU THINK?

Should governments put more money toward helping scientists investigate ideas such as string theory?

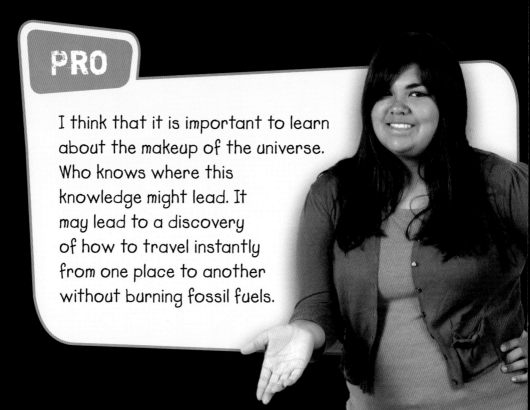

PRO

I think that it is important to learn about the makeup of the universe. Who knows where this knowledge might lead. It may lead to a discovery of how to travel instantly from one place to another without burning fossil fuels.

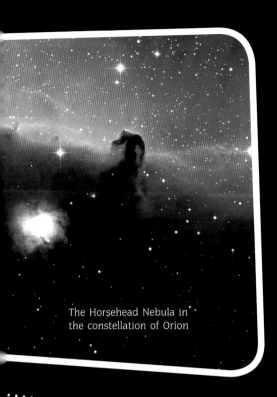

The Horsehead Nebula in the constellation of Orion

Astronomers are developing increasingly powerful telescopes that allow them to see farther into the universe than ever before. These scientists are often limited not just by human knowledge, but also by a lack of funds. The equipment they need often costs billions of dollars. Sometimes this money comes from government funds. At other times, wealthy organizations help out.

CON

We don't need to know everything about how the universe works, in order to live happy lives. Most of us won't understand it anyway. I think it is more important that we put research money to other causes, such as curing deadly diseases.

GLOSSARY

Astronomers

astrology (*uh STROL uh jee*) the study of how the positions of stars and planets supposedly affect people's lives

astronomer a scientist who studies the stars, planets, and space

bacteria (*bak TEER ee yuh*) tiny living things too small to be seen without a microscope

circumference (*ser KUM fer uhnss*) the distance around a circle or sphere

elliptical (*ee LIP tih kuhl*) shaped like an oval

erosion the wearing away of land by water or wind

friction (*FRIK shuhn*) the force that slows down an object whenever it touches something else, such as a surface

geometry (*jee OM uh tree*) the branch of math that deals with lines, angles, and shapes

humor one of the four liquids that were once believed to control the functions of the body

logical to do with logic, which is thinking that involves figuring things out in an ordered, step-by-step way

medium a substance, such as air or water, that surrounds things and in which those things exist

navigation the traveling of a particular course

nucleus (*NOO klee uhss*) the center of an atom, which is the tiniest amount of an element that still has the properties of that element

orbit to move in a regular path around something, especially a planet, the sun, or another heavenly body

philosopher (*fih LOSS uh fer*) a person who studies truth, wisdom, and the nature of reality

phlegm (*FLEM*) a thick liquid often coughed up as a symptom of a cold

physician (*fuh ZISH uhn*) a medical doctor

Renaissance (*REN uh sahnts*) a period in European history that lasted from the 1300s until about 1600. It was marked by advances in art, literature, and science.

simulate to copy or imitate

spherical (*SFEER ih kuhl*) sphere-shaped; shaped like a ball with all points on the surface the same distance from the center

translation a document that was first written in another language

FIND OUT MORE

BOOKS

Adasiewicz, Sue. *Mysterious Places*. Scholastic Inc., 2008.

Glass, Susan. *Analyze This!: Understanding the Scientific Method*. Heinemann Library, 2006.

Krull, Kathleen. *Isaac Newton*. Viking, 2006.

Platt, Richard. *Eureka!: Great Inventions and How They Happened*. Kingfisher, 2003.

Swanson, Diane. *Nibbling on Einstein's Brain: The Good, the Bad and the Bogus in Science*. Annick Press, 2001.

Whiting, Jim. *The Life and Times of Aristotle*. Blackwell Science, 2007.

WEB SITES

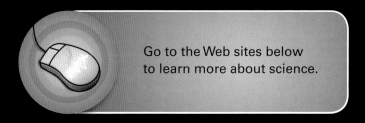

Go to the Web sites below to learn more about science.

www.sciencenewsforkids.org

www.biology4kids.com/files/studies_scimethod.html

www.historyforkids.org/learn/science

www.ology.amnh.org/einstein

INDEX

alchemy	20–21, 23	Galilei, Galileo	16–17
Aristotle	12–14, 17, 20	math	17, 22, 24
atoms	7, 21, 30–32	medicine	18–19, 28
chemistry	20–21, 28	Middle East	8, 14–15
dangers	27–29	navigation	10–11, 24
Einstein, Albert	22, 30–31	Newton, Isaac	22–23
errors	9, 12–13, 20, 27	Ptolemy	8, 15
experiments	12–13, 16–21, 24–29	reasoning	25

ABOUT THE AUTHOR

Mary Atkinson is the author of many fiction and nonfiction books for children. She has worked as a writer and editor for eighteen years. She also has a degree in biochemistry. Mary is fascinated with the way our understanding of our world and the universe has changed over the centuries. She hopes that readers will realize that it is always hard for people to know which new ideas are correct and which are not. And she hopes that readers will be inspired to keep open but discerning minds as we all move into the future and perhaps discover things that are currently beyond our imagination.